Where Does It Go?

# Where Does Recycling Go?

by Charlie W. Sterling

**Bullfrog Books**

# Ideas for Parents and Teachers

Bullfrog Books let children practice reading informational text at the earliest reading levels. Repetition, familiar words, and photo labels support early readers.

## Before Reading
- Discuss the cover photo. What does it tell them?
- Look at the picture glossary together. Read and discuss the words.

## Read the Book
- "Walk" through the book and look at the photos. Let the child ask questions. Point out the photo labels.
- Read the book to the child, or have him or her read independently.

## After Reading
- Prompt the child to think more. Ask: Do you recycle? Do you know what those items can be made into?

Bullfrog Books are published by Jump!
5357 Penn Avenue South
Minneapolis, MN 55419
www.jumplibrary.com

Library of Congress Cataloging-in-Publication Data

Names: Sterling, Charlie W., author.
Title: Where does recycling go? / by Charlie W. Sterling.
Description: Minneapolis: Jump!, [2021]
Series: Where does it go? | Includes index.
Audience: Ages 5–8. | Audience: Grades K–1.
Identifiers: LCCN 2020000287 (print)
LCCN 2020000288 (ebook)
ISBN 9781645275534 (hardcover)
ISBN 9781645275541 (paperback)
ISBN 9781645275558 (ebook)
Subjects: LCSH: Recycling (Waste, etc.)
Juvenile literature.
Classification: LCC TD794.5 .S745 2021 (print)
LCC TD794.5 (ebook) | DDC 628.4/458—dc23
LC record available at https://lccn.loc.gov/2020000287
LC ebook record available at https://lccn.loc.gov/2020000288

Editor: Jenna Gleisner
Designer: Molly Ballanger

Photo Credits: Michael Burrell/iStock, cover; matteodestafano/iStock, 1; Rawpixel/iStock, 3; vystekimages/Shutterstock, 4; ranplett/iStock, 5, 22tl; neenawat/iStock, 6–7; Jorgefontestad/iStock, 8–9, 23br; Rob Crandall/Shutterstock, 10–11, 22tr; Jim West/age fotostock/SuperStock, 12–13, 22br, 23bl; Biosphoto/SuperStock, 14, 22bm, 23tl; Akkalak Aiempradit/Shutterstock, 15, 22bl; liquid studios/Shutterstock, 16–17; RecycleMan/iStock, 18; all_about_people/Shutterstock, 19; Simba3003/Dreamstime, 20; Belish/Shutterstock, 20–21; Benoit Daoust/Shutterstock, 23tr; Gemenacom/Shutterstock, 24.

Printed in the United States of America at Corporate Graphics in North Mankato, Minnesota.

# Table of Contents

# New Items

Jon pours milk.
The jug is empty.
What does he do?

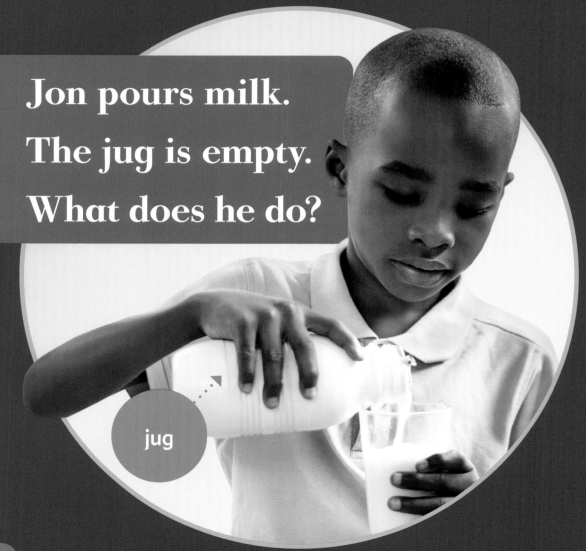

jug

He recycles it!

Why?

It is not trash.

recycling bin

5

landfill

Trash piles up.
Ew!
We can make less.
How?

We recycle!
What?
Many things!

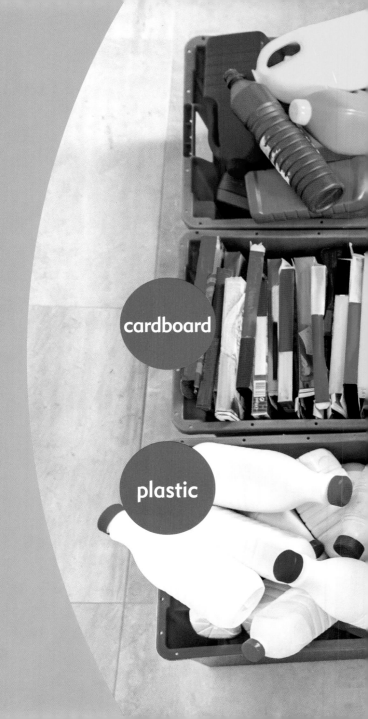

cardboard

plastic

metal

paper

glass

9

bin

collector

We put them in a bin.

The bin is picked up.

It goes to a plant.

It is sorted.

recycling
plant

13

paper
bundle

**Paper goes in bundles.**

It makes new paper!
Neat!

15

bridge

Metal is melted.
It makes new things.
Like what?
Bridges!

# Plastic is cut up.

plastic chips

Pieces are melted.

Why?

To make new items.

Like this!

playground set

19

# Glass is crushed.
# It can make beads.
# Wow!

glass bead

glass
pieces

# Where Recycling Goes

**What happens to recycling after it leaves your home? Take a look!**

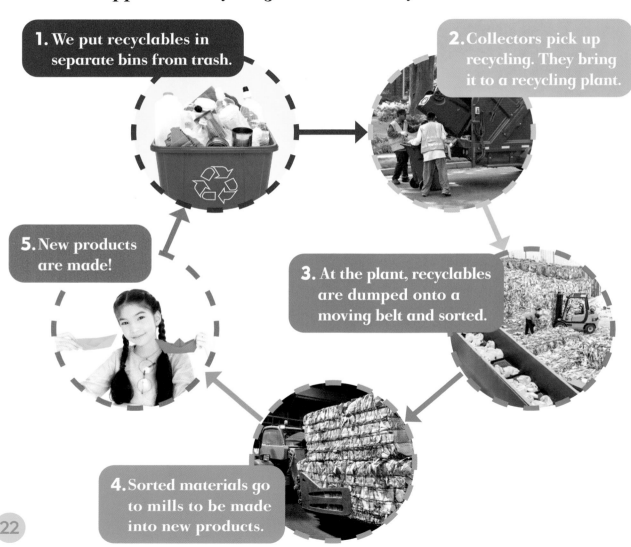

**1.** We put recyclables in separate bins from trash.

**2.** Collectors pick up recycling. They bring it to a recycling plant.

**3.** At the plant, recyclables are dumped onto a moving belt and sorted.

**4.** Sorted materials go to mills to be made into new products.

**5.** New products are made!

# Picture Glossary

**bundles**
Groups of things fastened together for easier handling.

**melted**
Changed something from a solid to a liquid by heating it.

**plant**
A building and the equipment inside that carry out a process.

**recycles**
Sends old items, such as glass, plastic, paper, aluminum, and tin cans, to be made into new items.

# Index

# To Learn More

**FACT SURFER**

**Finding more information is as easy as 1, 2, 3.**

❶ Go to www.factsurfer.com

❷ Enter "wheredoesrecyclinggo" into the search box.

❸ Choose your book to see a list of websites.